I Spy Thanksgiving

This Book Belongs To

_____

_____

_____

I Spy With My Little Eye Something Beginning With...

A Is For

acorn

B Is For

ball

I Spy With My Little Eye Something Beginning With...

C Is For

corn

I Spy With My Little Eye
Something Beginning With...

D Is For

dog

I Spy With My Little Eye
Something Beginning With...

E Is For

elephant

F Is For

fish

I Spy With My Little Eye
Something Beginning With...

G Is For

grapes

I Spy With My Little Eye Something Beginning With...

H Is For
House

I Spy With My Little Eye
Something Beginning With...

I Is For

ice cream

I Spy With My Little Eye Something Beginning With...

J Is For

Jelly

jelly

I Spy With My Little Eye
Something Beginning With...

K Is For

kettle

L Is For

leaf

I Spy With My Little Eye
Something Beginning With...

M Is For
mushroom

I Spy With My Little Eye Something Beginning With...

N

I Spy With My Little Eye
Something Beginning With...

O Is For

orange

I Spy With My Little Eye Something Beginning With...

I Spy With My Little Eye
Something Beginning With...

Q Is For

quack

I Spy With My Little Eye
Something Beginning With...

R Is For

rose

I Spy With My Little Eye
Something Beginning With...

S Is For

sweet potato

I Spy With My Little Eye
Something Beginning With...

T Is For

turkey

I Spy With My Little Eye
Something Beginning With...
U

U Is For

umbrella

I Spy With My Little Eye Something Beginning With...

V Is For

vegetables

I Spy With My Little Eye
Something Beginning With...

W Is For

wheel

I Spy With My Little Eye Something Beginning With...

X Is For

x-mas

I Spy With My Little Eye
Something Beginning With...

Y Is For

yeanling

I Spy With My Little Eye
Something Beginning With...

Z Is For

zucchini

Made in the USA
Las Vegas, NV
14 November 2024

11806388R00031